Yesterday & Today

TRADE AND COMMERCE

Lucile Davis

BLACKBIRCH®
PRESS

THOMSON
★
GALE

San Diego • Detroit • New York • San Francisco • Cleveland • New Haven, Conn. • Waterville, Maine • London • Munich

For more information, contact
The Gale Group, Inc.
27500 Drake Rd.
Farmington Hills, MI 48331-3535
Or you can visit our Internet site at http://www.gale.com

Picture Credits

Cover: © Art Today, Inc. (both)
© Archivo Iconografico, S.A./CORBIS, 7 (inset), 19 (bottom)
© Art Today, Inc, 10 (bottom), 17, 18, 26, 28
© Bettmann/CORBIS, 5, 6, 7 (top), 22 (top), 24, 27
© Blackbirch Press, 25, 28 (top), 31
© Chase Studio/ Phor Researchers, Inc., 4
© COREL Corporation, 11, 23
© Angelo Hornak/CORBIS, 15
© K.J. Historical/CORBIS, 29 (bottom)
© Erich Lessing/Art Resource, 12
Courtesy of Microsoft Archives and Lakeside School, 30
© National Archives, 20, 22 (bottom)
© North Wind Picture Archives, 8, 9, 10 (top), 13, 16
© Gianni Dagli Orti/CORBIS, 19 (top)
© Royal Ontario Museum/CORBIS, 7 (bottom)

LIBRARY OF CONGRESS CATALOGING-IN-PUBLICATION DATA

Davis, Lucile.
  Trade and commerce / by Lucile Davis.
    p. cm. — (Yesterday and today)
  Includes bibliographical references and index.
  ISBN 1-56711-829-1 (hardback: alk. paper)
  I. Commerce—History—Juvenile literature. Title. II. Series.

  HF353.D27 2004
  381'.09—dc22

                                                2004008271

Printed in the United States
10 9 8 7 6 5 4 3 2 1

Table of Contents

Before Trade

Prehistoric people were completely self-sufficient and knew how to use raw materials such as animal hides and carcasses to make food, clothing, and shelter.

Ever since a prehistoric hunter traded a chunk of meat for a neighbor's sack of fruit and nuts, humans have been involved in trade. Before then, people living in prehistoric times were self-sufficient. There were no markets or stores. People had to spend every day working to find food, shelter, and hides for clothes. Whatever they needed was free, but they had to work every waking hour to turn raw materials into useful things. When they could no longer find enough plants and animals to eat, people had to travel to another place to find food.

Eventually, people learned how to plant seeds and grow crops. They also learned they could breed and domesticate, or tame, animals and keep them nearby. This allowed people to stay in one place. They built houses and villages and

500 B.C.

100 B.C.

A.D. 100

200

500

1000

1200

1300

1400

1500

1600

1700

1800

1900

2000

2100

began to work together. While some people worked to raise food, others spent time making cloth or building houses and furniture. By working together, people found they could produce a surplus of food and goods. The surplus allowed people in one village to trade for things they did not have. A village that harvested a lot of grain could trade the surplus with a village that had raised a large herd of goats.

Cooperating to produce food and build homes made it possible for some people to have free time to do other things. Some learned how to weave grasses into mats. Others discovered how to sew shells and stones on clothing to create designs. This freedom to learn, discover, and create also allowed people the time to develop tools to help them do their work.

As people learned to work cooperatively to raise crops and build homes and villages, they developed tools, such as this sled made out of tree trunks, to help them.

Tools

Tools helped people work better and faster. They also helped people produce more food and goods for trade.

The first simple tools were made from sticks, bones, and stones. People sharpened small rocks by chipping away pieces until the stones had points. Farmers used sharp stones as hoes. They were also used as axes for cutting down trees. Hunters used sharp stones as knives to skin animals. Sharp stones and bones attached to sticks or tree limbs helped people hunt fish, plant seeds, and make clothing. These tools, however, were easily broken.

People learned to make tools with bronze and iron about 3500 B.C. Iron tools were harder and lasted longer than bronze. Metal tools could be created for specific jobs. For example, large knives were used to hunt and skin animals. People used smaller knives to carve wood and stone.

Metal tools lasted longer. This allowed individuals to become highly skilled at using them. With a sharp metal axe, a person could do a better job of cutting trees and turning the wood into furniture. A small metal knife allowed a craftsman to carve finer, more beautiful designs into wooden furniture. A craftsman known for making beautiful furniture found that people would travel a long way to trade for his work.

A good craftsman could trade for whatever he wanted or needed. A man skilled at fishing could

At first, people made simple tools by chipping rocks into sharp instruments that they could use as hoes, axes, or knives.

The Importance of Tools

Metal tools were so important they became valuable. In China, tools were traded for goods and services. About 1100 B.C., metalworkers began to make miniature tools that were used as money.

Prehistory ——

500 B.C. ——

100 B.C. ——

A.D. 100 ——

200 ——

500 ——

1000 ——

1200 ——

1300 ——

1400 ——

1500 ——

1600 ——

1700 ——

1800 ——

1900 ——

2000 ——

2100 ——

trade some of his catch for a craftsman's goods. There had to be agreement about how many fish were needed in exchange for a finely carved piece of furniture. This was decided by barter.

During the Bronze Age, people began to make tools with iron and bronze. Metal tools ranged from simple axes (inset) to more advanced items like the Chinese weaponry pictured below.

Ages of Toolmaking

Historians divide periods of human development based on toolmaking. These periods are the Stone Age (began 10,000 B.C.), the Bronze Age (started 3500 B.C.), the Iron Age (began between 1500 and 1000 B.C.), and the Age of Steel (started A.D. 1700).

Barter

Barter is the exchange of goods without money. A trade is completed when both parties are satisfied with the exchange.

People bartered for things they wanted but did not have. A farmer might barter a basket of wheat for a shepherd's sack of wool. The size of the basket or sack did not matter. If the two people agreed, the trade was completed.

Not all trades were that easy. If the shepherd did not need a basket of wheat, he might want to trade for berries instead. This required the farmer to gather berries himself or trade his wheat for someone's else's berries. Then he could make the trade with the shepherd.

The farmer who traded wheat for wool wanted cloth for clothing. Now that he had the wool, he needed it woven into cloth. If there were no weavers in his tribe, he had to go in search of one. He would then barter with the weaver. The farmer might be able to exchange the wool for cloth the weaver had already made. If the weaver had too much wool, he might ask for some of the farmer's grain along with the raw wool. The two would barter until they reached an agreement.

Because of the need to travel and barter with several people,

Early people, like the Aztec Indians depicted in this woodcut, bartered for a variety of goods, including food, animals, and cloth.

This woodcut from the Middle Ages shows farmers as they barter to trade lambs for a merchant's cloth. Once two people agreed to trade, they could exchange goods.

Prehistory

500 B.C.

100 B.C.

A.D. 100

200

500

1000

1200

1300

1400

1500

1600

1700

1800

1900

2000

2100

the farmer's trade might take a long time. To shorten the time and reduce the travel, people began to gather where two roads crossed to make their trades. These trading places also sprang up on seacoasts and in large towns. These places were called markets.

Modern-day Barter

Small businesses find each other on the Internet and organize into a trade group to barter for the exchange goods and services. For example, a printer might want to make calendars with the name of his or her print shop on them to use as advertising giveaways. A paper provider has the same idea. the printer and paper provider find each other through an Internet trade group. They barter on the amount of paper and who will pay the shipping costs. When the agreement is reached, they trade printing for paper so both will have advertising calendars.

Markets

Markets were created when people came together to buy, sell, or exchange goods and services. When people began to live in villages and towns, markets became a standard part of these settlements. Farmers, hunters, and shepherds would bring their produce or animals to a town market. There, they would trade for goods made by the townspeople, such as furniture, cloth, and pottery.

As towns grew, so did their markets. With more people gathered to trade, the exchange of goods changed. In early times, there had been no agreement on what things were worth. People simply traded what they had for what they needed. Markets allowed people to compare what they had to what others had. People were also able to shop around. If one fisherman's catch did not look good, a trader could find another fisherman with a better catch.

Left: Merchants, farmers, and hunters traveled to town markets to trade their goods. Below: When marketplace exchanges became more complicated, scribes (seated center) recorded written records of the trade.

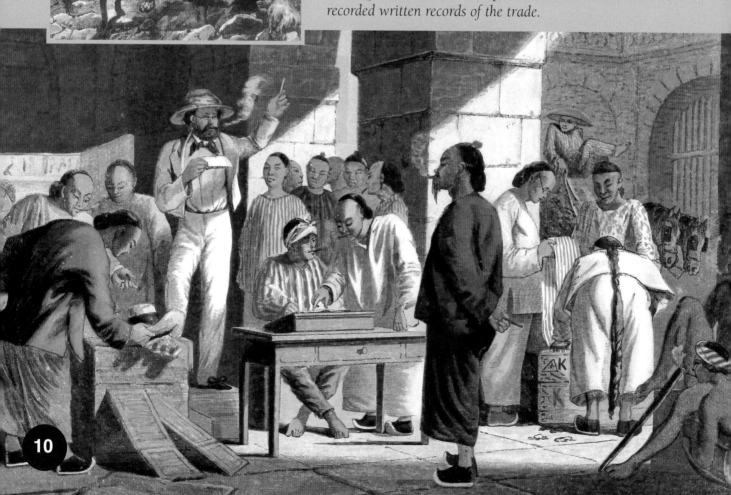

Prehistory ⎯

500 B.C. ⎯

100 B.C. ⎯

A.D. 100 ⎯

200 ⎯

500 ⎯

1000 ⎯

1200 ⎯

1300 ⎯

1400 ⎯

1500 ⎯

1600 ⎯

1700 ⎯

1800 ⎯

1900 ⎯

2000 ⎯

2100 ⎯

The better catch was worth more. People began to assign a value to their goods. The fisherman with the better catch could barter for more goods in exchange for his fish.

The larger the markets grew, the more complicated the exchanges became. Fifty bags of grain might be exchanged for hundreds of baskets. It became necessary to keep track of the exchanges through written records. A scribe would record an exchange with the names of the two people making the deal, the kind and amount of goods traded, and the date. A copy of the written record was given to each of the traders. The scribe kept a copy to be given to the tax collector. These early records were the first receipts and bills of sale.

It was difficult to exchange large amounts of goods. Hundreds of baskets would be hard to carry around a marketplace to trade for something else. Soon the receipt from the original exchange became a representation of the baskets. The trader who wanted to exchange the baskets for something else, had only to carry the receipt instead of all the baskets. This written record of sale became a form of money. Soon money became the method of exchange for all goods and services.

People can still buy local crafts and foods in the open-air mercados *of Mexican villages.*

Mexican Markets

Mercado means "market" in Spanish. In Mexico, open-air *mercados* are often found in village squares where local food and crafts can be bought along with manufactured goods. In the United States, *mercados* are large indoor or outdoor markets that sell Mexican food and goods that cannot be found in U.S. stores.

11

Ingots, like those pictured on the table in this carving, were the first metal money and varied in size, shape, and parity.

Money

Money is anything people accept in exchange for the things they sell or the work they do. In early times, objects used as money were usually things people considered valuable. Cattle, salt, beads, and metals have all been used as money. From prehistoric times, the most common form of money was gold and silver because these metals were hard to find.

The first metal money were lumps of metal called ingots. They came in various sizes and shapes, and their value was determined by weight. Some gold or silver ingots were not as pure as others, however. To solve this problem, people began to mint money. A minter would melt the precious metal and remove the impurities. Then he would pour the hot metal into molds to create round metal discs called coins. Each mold created a coin of a certain size and weight. Before the metal cooled completely, the minter would place his stamp on it. This stamp represented the minter's guarantee of the coin's purity and weight.

At first, the quality of work done by minters was not regulated. Traders soon learned which minters produced the purest coins. The coins of minters with the best reputation for purity held more value. Soon governments

Early Paper Money

In the eleventh century, Chinese bankers began to issue paper notes as receipts for the deposit of metal coins. These notes were the first paper money. Chinese coins were made of iron and very heavy. Paper notes were easier to carry.

began to regulate the making of money, and traders learned which government produced the purest money. These coins were valued above others. If the government minting the coins was stable, the money became even more valuable.

Money made trading over long distances easier. Coins were more convenient to carry than large sacks of wool or baskets of grain for barter. Money also enabled a trader to set the price of his goods so there was no need for long barter sessions. A trader might begin his journey with a set number of goods. Along his route, he would sell his wares and buy other things he believed he could sell along the way. A trader could travel a long distance buying and selling goods as he went. As more people began to trade over distances, they created roads and trails that crossed continents. These roads and trails became known as trade routes.

Individual minters began to put their stamp on the coins they made as a guarantee of purity and weight.

Prehistory —

500 B.C. —

100 B.C. —

A.D. 100 —

200 —

500 —

1000 —

1200 —

1300 —

1400 —

1500 —

1600 —

1700 —

1800 —

1900 —

2000 —

2100 —

Land Trade Routes

Land trade routes made it easier to move goods from place to place. These routes not only improved trade between cities, but also between civilizations.

Trade became so important to a civilization's success that some individuals worked at nothing but trading. These people were known as merchants. Historians recognize the Babylonians (2000 B.C. to 689 B.C.) as successful merchants. They traveled the land routes on foot or rode on mules. The Roman Empire (753 B.C. to A.D. 476) paved the roads that radiated out from Rome, its capital, in all directions. This promoted trade and made travel easier and faster. Merchants from faraway places made their way to Rome to trade. They brought gold and ivory from Africa, tin and slaves from Britain, gems and cloth from the Middle East, and silk from China.

Silk became a prized item. The Chinese were the first to learn how to produce silk and they guarded their secret for almost two thousand years. The only known route to China was overland through the Himalayan mountain range, which separated China from the Middle East. As a result, silk was expensive. To emperors and kings, however, no expense was too great to obtain the prized cloth. The demand for silk sent merchants from Europe to China and back beginning around 100 B.C. A number of trade routes

Babylonians were successful merchants who established land routes as early as 200 B.C.

Some roads built by the ancient Romans still exist today.

Prehistory —

500 B.C. —

100 B.C. —

A.D. 100 —

200 —

500 —

1000 —

1200 —

1300 —

1400 —

1500 —

1600 —

1700 —

1800 —

1900 —

2000 —

2100 —

were created between Europe and China. They were called the Silk Road.

After the fall of the Roman Empire in A.D. 476, international trade declined, although merchant caravans still made the trip across the mountains to China. But international trade revived after Marco Polo and other European merchants made their way to eastern Asia to trade for Chinese goods. This trade revival began about A.D. 1100 when Italy began to build large fleets of ships to carry goods from country to country.

Roman Roads

The ancient Roman government constructed roads that covered fifty thousand miles. Built to speed the movement of troops throughout the empire, the roads also promoted trade and communication. The roads built by the Roman Empire were so important to European trade that the brick-paved highways were maintained long after the empire collapsed. In fact, some Roman roads still exist.

Merchants from the wealthy Roman Empire used their ships to establish trade with most of the world, making Rome the center of international trade for hundreds of years.

Sea Trade

Sea trade has been an important part of trade and commerce since early times. Sometime after 5000 B.C., the Sumerians and Egyptians built boats and began to trade with each other. The Phoenicians were known as good sailors and honest traders. Around 1000 B.C., they set sail from their home port on the coast of Lebanon to trade with cities along the Mediterranean Sea. The Greeks and Romans joined the Mediterranean Sea trade. The large and wealthy Roman Empire drew merchant ships, as well as land traders, from most of the world. Rome was the world center for trade until the empire collapsed in A.D. 476. The loss of this large trade center effectively shut down international trade for over a thousand years.

In 1095, Pope Urban II called for a crusade, or holy war, against the Muslims to win back the Holy Land, Palestine. The shipowners of Genoa, Pisa, and Venice provided the European holy warriors with transportation across the Mediterranean. They were rewarded with trade concessions, or special rights to trade, in the conquered Muslim lands. It gave the Italian traders direct access to the trade routes of Asia.

The Crusades and the resulting trade with the East created a demand for Asian goods in Europe. This demand drove shippers to look for faster sea routes to the Indies, which included India, China, the East Indies, and Japan. The need for a faster route to the East led an Italian captain sailing for Portugal to make a plan. Christopher Columbus believed he could sail west around the world to reach the Indies. The Portuguese king would not fund Columbus's voyage, but the Spanish monarchs Ferdinand and Isabella did. Columbus did not reach the Indies in 1492, because two large continents, North and South America, blocked his way. The discovery of these new lands led to wealth for European nations. After the Americas were colonized and new nations established, international trade once again flourished. Raw materials from the Americas were shipped to Europe in exchange for manufactured goods sent from Europe to the Americas.

FAST FACT

Caravel sailing ships built by the Portuguese were favored by traders and discoverers who sailed the world beginning in A.D. 1300. The caravels were smaller, sturdier, and faster than the Spanish-built galleons.

While European holy warriors fought in the Crusades (pictured), the Italian shipowners who transported them to Palestine received special rights to trade in the newly conquered lands.

Prehistory

500 B.C.

100 B.C.

A.D. 100

200

500

1000

1200

1300

1400

1500

1600

1700

1800

1900

2000

2100

Manufacturing

The word *manufacture* comes from two Latin words—*manus*, meaning "hand", and *facere*, meaning "to make". Originally, to manufacture something meant to make it by hand. Later it came to mean making something by hand or machine.

As demand for manufactured goods increased, workers moved their work out of their homes and into shops. In large cities, workers who produced the same type of item often had shops on the same street. These streets were often named after the businesses on them. Many cities had a Weaver Street or a Potter Street.

By the Middle Ages (about A.D. 476 to the 1400s), merchants and craftsmen in Europe and the Middle East formed associations called guilds. Merchant guilds controlled the prices and trade of goods in their street or city. Craft guilds oversaw the quality of production and protected the rights of the workers.

Guild members and home-based workers continued to be the main source of manufactured goods until the 1700s. Before 1750, some manufacturing was done under the domestic system. A businessman, known as the organizer, would buy raw materials and hand them out to home workers, who would make the product. Later he would go back to collect the manufactured product and pay the workers. The products were then sold to merchants. The domestic

Manufactured goods such as books were made by hand in homes or small shops until the 1700s.

18

system was the beginning of managed manufacturing. It was replaced by the Industrial Revolution, during which workers were drawn out of their homes and into factories to mass-produce goods.

Guilds

Many historians believe the craft guilds organized in the Middle Ages were the forerunners of modern labor unions. These workers' unions began to organize in Europe in the early 1800s.

Workers' guilds were organized in the Ottoman Empire beginning around the fourteenth century. These guilds were much like the craft guilds formed in Europe at about the same time.

Prehistory ——

500 B.C. ——

100 B.C. ——

A.D. 100 ——

200 ——

500 ——

1000 ——

1200 ——

1300 ——

1400 ——

1500 ——

1600 ——

1700 ——

1800 ——

1900 ——

2000 ——

2100 ——

19

Industrial Revolution

The Industrial Revolution began in England in the 1760s. It was the beginning of large-scale, mechanized manufacturing. Three things came together to create this revolution—machines, money, and market demand.

During the 1600s, men made many new mechanical inventions, but most were more for play than practical use. Windup toys and watches amazed the public but did little to advance trade and commerce. That changed when wealthy people began to look for profitable ways to invest their money. The answer appeared in the 1690s when Europeans became fond of cotton cloth from India. To protects its own textile, or cloth manufacturing, industry, the British Parliament closed off the importation of cloth

During the Industrial Revolution, even children went to work in factories to keep up with the demand for cotton clothing and other goods.

Prehistory ——

500 B.C. ——

100 B.C. ——

A.D. 100 ——

200 ——

500 ——

1000 ——

1200 ——

1300 ——

1400 ——

1500 ——

1600 ——

1700 ——

1800 ——

1900 ——

2000 ——

2100 ——

from India. The rich then invested in the emerging British
textile industry. Inventors turned their efforts to building
machines for the new industry.

By 1750, British textile manufacturers could not keep up
with the demand for cotton cloth. They offered a prize to
anyone who could invent a machine that could spin cotton
fibers into yarn or thread. Over the next one hundred
years, a number of machines, such as the spinning jenny
and the spinning mule, were invented to improve textile
making. Since one machine could do the work of many
workers, these machines shortened the time it took to
manufacture cotton cloth and reduced the cost. The success
of the English textile industry led farmers in the United
States to settle in the southern part of North America,
where cotton could be easily grown. In 1793, American Eli
Whitney added his cotton gin, a mechanical device that
pulled seeds from cotton, to the list of machines invented
to support the textile industry.

Cotton clothing was not the only item in demand during
the 1700s. Pottery, iron cooking pots, and bricks were also
in demand. This led to the development of the factory
system. Workers were hired to manufacture items in one
place under the direction of a manager. Inventors
continued to create machines to help factory workers
produce more goods at a faster rate. These machines
brought about mass production.

FAST FACT

James Hargreaves of
Lancashire, England,
invented the spinning
jenny in 1764. It could
spin sixteen or more
threads at one time.
The name *jenny* came
from *gin*, the local word
for *engine*.

Mass Production

Mass production is the large-scale manufacturing of machines or other goods in standard sizes. Mass-produced goods can be made faster and at lower cost. Eli Whitney, the inventor of the cotton gin, created the method for factory mass production.

In 1798, the United States needed to build up its army, but gunsmiths could not supply enough arms for the soldiers. Guns were created by hand, one at a time. This meant each gun was different. The government hired Whitney to make ten thousand muskets. He developed the machine tools that made the identical gun parts. Guns could then be mass-produced using the interchangeable parts.

A century later, Henry Ford improved the process of mass production. Ford manufactured automobiles. He and the other American automobile manufacturers produced cars only the wealthy could afford. Ford decided to create a more affordable automobile. The Model T Ford appeared in 1908. It was sturdy and cost less than one thousand dollars, but it was still too expensive for many people. Ford directed his managers to reduce costs. The most important cost-reducing method involved putting the automobile frame on a conveyor belt that moved the frame down a

Henry Ford's (above) assmebly line (right) reduced the time it took to produce a car from twelve and a half hours to an hour and a half.

In today's automobile factories, robots perform most of the mass-production work.

Prehistory ——

500 B.C. ——

100 B.C. ——

A.D. 100 ——

200 ——

500 ——

1000 ——

1200 ——

1300 ——

1400 ——

1500 ——

1600 ——

1700 ——

1800 ——

1900 ——

2000 ——

2100 ——

long line. As the frame moved by them, workers attached parts and tightened bolts. What started as a frame turned into a fully assembled automobile at the end of the assembly line. The assembly line not only reduced cost, it shortened the time it took to build the auto from twelve and a half worker hours to one and a half worker hours. Ford cars could then be sold at lower prices.

Mass production continues to be the assembly method used in modern factories. Today, however, much of the work is done by electric machines called robots.

Whitney's Interchangeable Parts

The U.S. government contracted Eli Whitney to manufacture ten thousand guns in two years, but he only produced five hundred in that time. Called to Washington to explain, Whitney assembled ten guns from piles of identical parts. He had spent two years developing the machine tools that made the identical gun parts. This led to mass production.

After Thomas Edison invented the electric light, factories could operate around the clock, increasing both production and the demand for goods and services.

Electricity

When humans learned to harness electricity, they were able to make their lives easier. Electricity also changed the way people conducted trade and commerce.

Practical uses for electricity were not discovered until the 1800s. Thomas Edison's electric light and his improvements to Alexander Graham Bell's telephone made a major change in trade and commerce.

In 1882, Edison and his engineers lit financier J.P. Morgan's mansion with three hundred lightbulbs to demonstrate the usefulness and brilliance of electric lighting. Soon homes, businesses, and factories began to use this new system of illumination instead of gaslights.

Electric lights were safer. Gaslights in a closed room produced a buildup of carbon monoxide fumes that choked workers. In textile factories, the open gas flames could ignite fires. With electric lights, factories could operate twenty-four hours a day and employ three shifts of workers. With more people earning money, the demand for goods and services increased. This led manufacturers to look for ways to increase production. Electricity provided the means.

Electric machines made manufacturing and the conducting of business easier and faster. They also replaced large numbers of workers, and that further reduced the cost of producing goods. Factories and offices were not the only places workers were needed, however. In order to grow and be profitable, businesses needed people who could transport materials and goods.

The gaslights that were used to illuminate textile factories before electric light was introduced sometimes caused huge fires like the one depicted here.

Big Names in Electricity

The names of many of the inventors who helped bring electricity into practical use are found in electric units of measure. An amp is a unit of measure for electrical current. Amp is short for ampere, and is named for André-Marie Ampère. He was a French physicist and mathematician who discovered the relationship between electrical currents and magnetic fields. Hertz is a unit for measuring the length of a vibrating energy wave. It is named after Heinrich R. Hertz, a German physicist who demonstrated how to generate and detect radio waves. A volt measures electrical current. It is named for Italian physicist Alessandro Volta, who first demonstrated the measurement.

Prehistory

500 B.C.

100 B.C.

A.D. 100

200

500

1000

1200

1300

1400

1500

1600

1700

1800

1900

2000

2100

Transportation

Transportation has always been a key part of trade and commerce. Early traders used slaves, pack animals, cattle-drawn carts, and boats to move goods to markets. These methods of transporting goods remained unchanged until 1800. In that year steam engines were placed in boats. This created a faster method of transportation. Steam engines also powered trains.

The invention of the internal combustion engine led to the next new method of transportation—automobiles and trucks. In the twentieth century, trucks first competed with railroads to move raw materials and goods from place to place. Soon, however, these two transport methods were combined to create an efficient movement of raw materials to factories and finished goods to market. Trailer trucks were loaded with goods and driven to train yards, where they were loaded onto flatbed railroad cars. This is called piggybacking. Trains still deliver truck trailers to major cities every day. When the trailers are unloaded, truck cabs hook on and drive the trailers to stores and warehouses.

Steam-powered trains were the primary way to transport raw material and finished goods over land until trucks and automobiles were introduced in the twentieth century.

In 1903, Orville and Wilbur Wright built and flew the first airplane. Soon airplanes joined trucks and railroads as a major part of the transportation system for trade and commerce. The development of jet-powered airplanes during World War II added speed to commercial transportation. Jet airplanes made it possible for people and goods to travel around the world in a matter of hours instead of days. The war in Europe and Asia created air routes for the transport of men and supplies to the fighting fronts. After the war, these air routes became the new worldwide air trade routes.

In the last half of the twentieth century, the demand for goods and services was worldwide. The challenge to trade and commerce was how to connect buyers and sellers. A new industry, marketing, developed to handle this challenge.

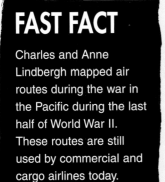

FAST FACT

Charles and Anne Lindbergh mapped air routes during the war in the Pacific during the last half of World War II. These routes are still used by commercial and cargo airlines today.

Charles and Anne Lindbergh mapped Pacific air routes for the Allies during World War II. Today, those same routes are used by commercial and cargo airlines.

Prehistory —

500 B.C. —

100 B.C. —

A.D. 100 —

200 —

500 —

1000 —

1200 —

1300 —

1400 —

1500 —

1600 —

1700 —

1800 —

1900 —

2000 —

2100 —

Marketing

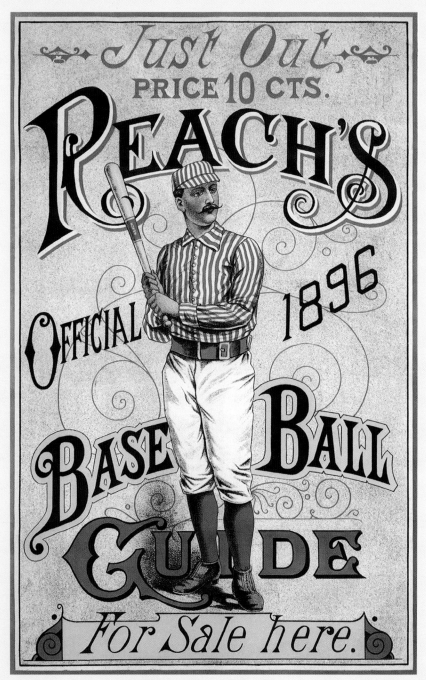

Advertisements designed to grab a potential consumer's attention appeared as early as the 1800s.

The marketing industry helps connect buyers and sellers. The businesses that provide marketing services are advertisers or promoters, market researchers, and product developers.

Advertisers and promoters make consumers aware of products and try to persuade them to buy. In the nineteenth and early twentieth centuries, advertising and promotion were handled by store sales staff or traveling salesmen. Store salespeople were given bonuses for introducing and selling new products. Traveling salesmen made money by earning a percentage of their sales, which is called a commission. To advertise the products they sold, some salesmen in the 1800s traveled in wagons painted with pictures of their wares. Sometimes the salesman traveled with performers. When the painted sales wagon stopped, the performers gave a show to attract an audience of possible customers.

After World War II, advertising was combined with entertainment on radio and television. Advertisements on radio and television shows had to compete with the entertainment for the audience's attention. This led to the need for companies that could produce attention-grabbing ads. These advertising agencies also produced print ads for newspapers, magazines, and catalogs.

For your country's sake today—

For your own sake tomorrow

transistors **PHILIPS**

A patriotic World War II advertisement (top) urges women to join the military while a more contemporary ad for a radio reflects a more peaceful time.

Market researchers studied what consumers liked or disliked about products. They also tried to find out what new items customers wanted. Product developers would then create new products based on what market research revealed about the buying public's demands. By the late 1990s, marketing had moved into a new, computerized medium known as the Internet.

Prehistory —

500 B.C. —

100 B.C. —

A.D. 100 —

200 —

500 —

1000 —

1200 —

1300 —

1400 —

1500 —

1600 —

1700 —

1800 —

1900 —

2000 —

2100 —

The World Wide Web

The Internet allows buyers and sellers all over the world to conduct trade and commerce instantly. It is a communications network that connects computers around the world. The Internet began as a communications tool of the U.S. military in the 1960s. By the 1980s, computer networks all over the world were linked to create the World Wide Web. Large companies, as well as small, one-person businesses, could have Web sites. This allowed them to do business with customers around the world twenty-four hours a day, seven days a week.

In the 1990s, Internet business boomed. People learned that setting up shop on the Internet was much cheaper than investing in a brick-and-mortar store in their

When Bill Gates (standing) was a student, no one imagined that trade and commerce would move into cyberspace within thirty years.

hometown. In addition, the Internet store could reach more people. It also had the potential to be more profitable.

At the beginning of the twenty-first century, almost anything could be bought through the Internet. It is the largest market in the world, and it has moved trade and commerce into cyberspace. The future of Internet trade and commerce is almost unlimited. Computer scientists and businesspeople predict another boom before the middle of the century. New processes will drive the boom. Three-dimensional pictures of products, called holographs, will help customers see products more realistically. Soon, college degrees from respected universities will be offered through Internet classes. A person might even earn a degree in Internet trade and commerce.

No matter what the future brings, trade and commerce will always be important. From the days when people traded meat for fruit and nuts to today's bartering on the World Wide Web, trade and commerce has helped improve the quality of life for people all around the world.

Today, the World Wide Web is the largest marketplace in the world.

Amazon.com: Internet Shopping

In 1994, a man named Jeff Bezos discovered an important fact. Traffic on the Internet had increased 2,300 percent from its days as an information network for the government and universities. He opened an Internet site called Amazon.com to sell books. Amazon.com had no stores, only warehouses. Because Amazon.com did not have the expense of operating stores, it could offer books at a reduced price. The Amazon.com business model helped set online retailing in motion.

Prehistory ——

500 B.C. ——

100 B.C. ——

A.D. 100 ——

200 ——

500 ——

1000 ——

1200 ——

1300 ——

1400 ——

1500 ——

1600 ——

1700 ——

1800 ——

1900 ——

2000 ——

2100 ——

Glossary

barter: To trade by exchanging goods or services instead of using money.

commerce: The buying and selling of goods or commodities on a large scale that involves transportation from place to place.

conveyor belt: A moving belt that carries objects from one place to another in a factory.

database: Information that is organized and stored in a computer.

domestic: Related to the home. The domestic system involved manufacturing work being done in the home.

financier: One who raises and manages a large amount of money to invest in business.

holograph: An image made by laser beams that looks three-dimensional.

interchangeable: Easily switched; mutual substitution.

merchant: Someone who sells goods for profit.

minter: Someone who makes coins.

prehistoric: The time before history was recorded in writing.

radiate: To spread out from the center.

scribe: In early civilizations, someone who could write. In the Middle Ages, someone who copied books, contracts, and other documents.

textile: Fabric or cloth that has been woven or knitted.

transistor: Small electronic part that controls the flow of electric current in radios, televisions, computers, and other devices.

virtual: Almost real.

For More Information

Books

Jeanne Bendick and Robert Bendick, *Markets: From Barter to Bar Codes.* New York: Franklin Watts, 1997.

Claire Craig, *Explorers and Traders.* Alexandria, VA: Time-Life Books, 1996.

Geography Department of Runestone Press, *Sold! The Origins of Money and Trade.* Minneapolis, MN: Runestone Press, 1994.

Web Sites

The Artistry of African Currency (www.nmafa.si.edu). Interesting facts about the various materials and art of Africa's various rates of exchange.

Index